Kemps nine daies wonder

Performed in London t

GW00599433

Containing the pleasure, pa
of William Kemp betweene London and that Citty
in his late Morrice

Wherein is somewhat set downe worth note; to reproove
the slaunders spred of him: many things merry,
nothing hurtfull.

Drawings by Robert Yaxley

Typeset and published at the
Larks Press
Ordnance Farmhouse, Guist Bottom, Dereham, NR20 5PF
01328 829207

An earlier limited edition of 350 copies of Will Kemp's tale was
the very first publication of the Larks Press in 1985. It was
typeset by hand and printed on a Vicobold letterpress machine.
Since then we have never entirely ceased to receive orders for
the book, although it has long been out of print.

This new edition has been printed at the Lanceni Press,
Fakenham.

British Library Cataloguing-in-publication Data.
A catalogue record for this book is available at the
British Library.

© Editorial - Susan Yaxley, 1997

ISBN 0 948400 53 6

Editorial Note

Kemps nine daies wonder is Will Kemp's own account of his famous dance from London to Norwich. It was first published in the year 1600 to refute the highly-coloured and inaccurate versions of the story then being spread abroad by the ballad-mongers of the City (the sixteenth century equivalent of the tabloid press).

The intention of this new edition is to make Kemp's cheerful little tale available in a readily legible version with a short glossary to explain the few obscurities in the text. The original spelling has been retained, except that 'u's have been changed to 'v's and 'i's to 'j's where modern usage requires it. Abbreviated forms used in the original have also been expanded. The lay-out follows the spirit of the original typesetting without copying all its eccentricities.

Kemp actually performed his dance in the months of February and March, which in the old calendar would have been called 1599, the new year then beginning on March 25th. The exact dating of his dance is also complicated by the fact that 1600 was a leap year. The dating we have given is correct according to Cheney's *Handbook of Dates,* but it may be right to point out that we differ by one day from Chris Harris in his biography of Kemp, *Shakespeare's Forgotten Clown.*

S.Y. 1997

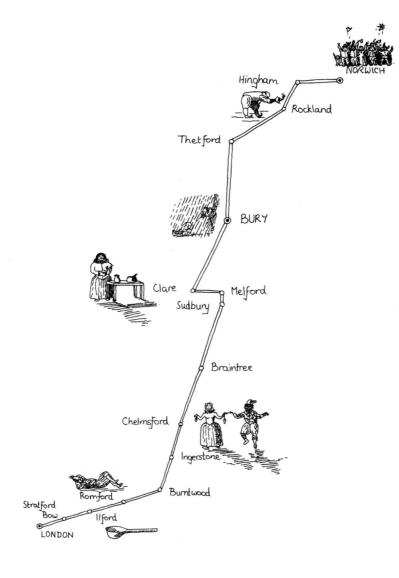

NORWICH

Hingham

Rockland

Thetford

BURY

Clare   Melford

Sudbury

Braintree

Chelmsford

Ingerstone

Romford   Burntwood

Stratford
Bow
LONDON   Ilford

Will Kemp

'Cavaliero Kemp, head-Master of Morrice-daunccrs,
high head borough of heighs, and onely tricker of your
trill-lilles..'

Will Kemp was a Londoner by birth, although there were
branches of the Kemp family in other parts of the country,
including Middlesex, Norfolk and Suffolk. At the time of his
great 'daunce' from London to Norwich he was already past his
fiftieth year and his reputation as a comedian had spread well
beyond the shores of Queen Elizabeth's England.

During the 1580s he travelled on the Continent,
especially in Germany and Denmark, with the Earl of Leicester's
players, and when he returned to England he was apprenticed
to the most famous comic actor of his day, Dick Tarleton.
When Tarleton died, in 1588, Kemp was his natural successor.
Thomas Nash, in the dedication of *'An Almond for a Parrat'*
describes Kemp as *'that most comicall and conceited cavaliere*
Monsieur du Kempe, Jest monger and Vice-gerent generall to
the Ghoste of Dicke Tarlton'.

In 1589 Kemp joined Edward Alleyn's company, known
as Lord Strange's men, and when London was free of plague,
they performed at the Rose theatre. When plague was about, as
in 1593, the theatres were closed and the players took to the
road and did the best they could in the provinces. They were
not always welcome, however, for they might be carrying the
plague with them. In 1594 Norwich City paid players not to act,
but to go away!

Back in London, Kemp moved from Edward Alleyn's
company to the Lord Chamberlain's Men, the company of
Richard Burbage and William Shakespeare which then held the
lease of 'The Theatre' in Shoreditch. For five years Kemp

worked in this illustrious company and is believed to have been the first actor to play Lancelot Gobbo in *'The Merchant of Venice'* and Dogberry in *'Much Ado about Nothing'* . The events of 1598, however, were to cause Kemp and Shakespeare to part company.

The lease of the Shoreditch site came to an end and the theatre itself had to be demolished in order to avoid its falling into the possession of the landlord. Burbage dismantled 'The Theatre' and rebuilt on the South Bank of the river, a smaller playhouse to be called 'The Globe', completed in 1599.

Kemp had gained a great reputation for his 'Jigs' which combined ribald verse, dance and song, and required all the skills of the stand-up comic, quickness of wit and the ability to milk an audience for all the laughs he could get. He was the darling of the 'groundlings'. This was both his strength and his weakness, for the growing Puritan sentiment of the times required that theatre should move up-market. Chris Harris in *'Shakespeare's Forgotten Clown'* has argued persuasively that Kemp's following was among the common folk, and his skills improvisatory, but Burbage and Shakespeare were moving towards a set text and an audience of gentlefolk. Whether voluntarily or not, Kemp left the Lord Chamberlain's Men in 1599 and sold his shares in the Globe. He was then out of work and probably in need of money.

Resourceful as ever, he decided to exploit his popularity and his dancing skill by a multiple wager. He laid bets with a number of Londoners that he could dance the 'Morrice' all the way from London to Norwich. If he succeeded, they were to repay him threefold. And so on the first Monday in Lent, 1599/1600, before 7 a.m., he met his servant George Bee, and his companions Thomas Slye the 'Taberer' and George Sprat who was to be 'overseer' or referee, and set out to dance from the house of Lord Mayor of London to that of the Mayor of Norwich.

THE EPISTLE DEDICATORY

*To the true Ennobled Lady, and his most bountifull Mistris,
Mistris Anne Fitton, Mayde of Honour
to the most sacred Mayde Royall Queene Elizabeth.*

Honorable Mistris in the waine of my litle wit, I am forst to desire your protection, else every Ballad-singer will proclaime me bankrupt of honesty. A sort of mad fellows seeing me merrily dispos'd in a Morrice, have so bepainted mee in print since my gambols began from London to Norwich, that (having but an ill face before) I shall appeare to the world without a face, if your fayre hand wipe not away their foule coulors. One hath written *Kemps farewell* to the tune of Kery, mery, Buffe: another his desperate daungers in his late travaile: the third his entertainment to New-market; which towne I came never neere by the length of halfe the heath. Some sweare in a Trenchmore I have trode a good way to winne the world: others that guesse righter, affirme, I have without good help daunst myselfe out of the world: many say many thinges that were never thought. But in a word your poore servant offers the truth of his progresse and profit to your honourable view, receive it I beseech you, such as it is, rude and plaine, for I know your pure judgement, lookes as soone to see beauty in a Blackamoore, or heare smooth speech from a Stammerer, as to finde any thing, but blunt mirth in a Morrice dauncer, especially such a one as *Will Kemp,* that has spent his life in mad Jigges and merry jestes. Three reasons moove mee to make publik this journey, one to reprove lying fooles I never knew: the other to commend loving friends, which by the way I daily found: the third to show my

1

duety to your honorable selfe, whose favours (among other bountifull friends) makes me (dispight of this sad world) judge my hart Corke, & my heeles feathers, so that methinks I could flye to Rome (at least hop to Rome, as the old Proverb is) with a morter on my head. In which light conceite I lowly begge pardon and leave, for my Tabrer strikes his huntsup, I must to Norwich: Imagine Noble Mistris, I am now setting from my Lord Mayors, the houre about seaven, the morning gloomy, the company many, my hart merry.

Your worthy Ladiships most
unworthy servant
William Kemp

Kemps nine dayes wonder:

Performed in a Morrice from London to Norwich

Wherein every dayes journey is pleasantly set downe,
to satisfie his friends the truth, against all lying Ballad-makers;
What he did, how hee was welcome, and by whom entertained

The first dayes journey, being the first Munday in cleane Lent, from the right honorable the Lord Mayors of London.

The first Munday in Lent, the close morning promising a cleere day, (attended on by **Thomas Slye** my Taberer, **William Bee** my servant, and **George Sprat,** appointed for my overseer, that I should take no other ease but my prescribed order) my selfe, thats I, otherwise called **Cavaliero Kemp,** head-Master of Morrice-dauncers, high head borough of heighs, and onely tricker of your Trill-lilles, and best bel-shangles betweene Sion and mount Surrey, began frolickly to foote it, from the right Honorable the Lord Mayors of London, towards the right worshipfull (and truely bountifull) Master Mayors of Norwich.

My setting forward was somewhat before seaven in the morning, my Taberer stroke up merrily, and as faste as kinde peoples thronging together would give mee leave, thorow

3

London I leapt; By the way many good olde people, and divers others of yonger yeeres, of meere kindnes, gave me bowd sixpences and grotes, blessing me with their harty prayers and God-speedes.

     Being past White chappell, and having left faire London, with all that North-east Suburb before named, multitudes of Londoners left not me: but eyther to keepe a custome which many holde, that Mile-end is no walke without recreation at Stratford Bow with Creame and Cakes, or else for love they beare toward me, or perhappes to make themselves merry, if I should chance (as many thought) to give over my Morrice within a mile of Mile-end. How ever, many a thousand brought me to Bow, where I rested a while from dauncing, but had small rest with those that would have urg'd me to drinking. But I warrant you **Will Kemp** was wise enough: to their ful cups, kinde thanks was my returne, with Gentlemanlike protestations: as, truely sir, I dare not: it stands not with the congruity of my health. Congruitie said I? how came that strange language in my mouth? I thinke scarcely that it is any Christen worde, and yet it mey be a good worde for ought I knowe, though I never made it, nor doe verye well understand it; yet I am sure I have bought it at the wordmongers, at as deare a rate, as I could have had a whole 100. of Bavines at the wood-mongers. Farwell Congruitie for I meane now to be more concise, and stand upon evener bases: but I must neither stand nor sit, the Tabrer strikes alarum. Tickle it, good Tom, Ile follow thee. Farwell Bowe, have over the Bridge, where I heard say, honest Conscience was once drownd. Its pittye if it were so: but thats no matter belonging to our Morrice, lets now along to Stratford Langton.

     Many good fellows being there met, and knowing how

4

well I loved the sporte, had prepared a Beare-bayting: but so unreasonable were the multitudes of people, that I could only heare the Beare roare, and the dogges howle: therefore forward I went with my hey de gaies to Ilford, where I againe rested, and was by the people of the towne and countrey there-about very very wel welcomd: being offred carowses in the great spoon, one whole draught being able at that time to have drawne my little wit drye: but being afrayde of the olde Proverbe (He had need of a long spoone that eats with the devil) I soberly gave my boone Companyons the slip.

From Ilford by Moone-shine, I set forward, dauncing within a quarter of a myle of Romford: where in the high way, two strong Jades (having belike some great quarrell to me unknowne) were beating & byting either of other. And such through Gods help was my good hap, that I escaped their hoofes, both being raysed with their fore feete over my head, like two Smithes over an Anvyle.

There being the end of my first dayes Morrice, a kinde Gentleman of London lighting from his horse, would have no nay but I should leap into his saddle. To be plaine with ye, I was not proud, but kindly tooke his kindlyer offer, chiefely thereto urg'd by my wearines: so I rid to my Inne at Romford.

In that towne, to give rest to my well labour'd limbes, I continued two dayes, being much beholding to the townsmen for their love, but more to the Londoners, that came hourely thither in great numbers to visite me: offring much more kindnes then I was willing to accept.

The second dayes journey, beeing Thursday of the first weeke.

Thursday being Market day at Burnt-wood, **Tom Slye** was earlyer up then the Lark, and sounded merrily the Morrice: I rowsed myselfe, and returned from Romford to the place where I tooke horse the first night, dauncing that quarter of a myle back againe thorow Romford, and so merrily to Burnt-wood: yet now I remember it well, I had no great cause of mirth, for at Romford townes end I strained my hip, and for a time endured exceeding paine: but being loath to trouble a Surgeon I held on, finding remedy by labour that had hurt mee, for it came in a turne, and so in my daunce I turned it out of my service againe.

The multitudes were so great at my comming to Burnt-wood, that I had much a doe (though I made many intreaties and staies) to get passage to my Inne.

In this towne two Cut-purses were taken, that with other two of their companions followed mee from London (as many better disposed persons did:) but these two dy-doppers gave out when they were apprehended, that they had laid wagers and betted about my journey. Whereupon the Officers bringing them to my Inne, I justly denyed their acquaintance, saving that I remembred one of them to be a noted Cut-purse, such a one as we tye to a poast on our stage, for all people to wonder at, when at a play they are taken pilfring.

This fellow & his half brother being found with the deed, were sent to Jayle: their other two consorts had the charity of the towne, & after a dance of Trenchmore at the whipping crosse, they were sent back to London: where I am afraide there are too many of their occupation. To be short I thought myself well rid of foure such followers, and I wish hartily that the whole world were cleer of such companions.

Having rested well at Burnt wood, the Moone shining clearely, and the weather being calme, in the evening I tript it to Ingerstone, stealing away from those numbers of people that followed mee: yet doe I what I could, I had above fiftie in the company, some of London, the other of the Country there about, that would needs when they heard my Taber, trudge after me through thicke and thin.

The third dayes journey, being Friday
of the first weeke

On Friday morning I set forward towardes Chelmsford, not having past two hundred, being the least company that I had in the day time: betweene London and that place. Onward I went thus easily followed, till I come to Witford-bridge where a number of country people, and many Gentlemen and Gentlewomen, were gathered together to see me. Sir Thomas Mildmay standing at his park pale, received gently a payre of garters of me: gloves, points, and garters, being my ordinary marchandize, that I put out to venter for performance of my merry voyage.

So much a doe I had to passe by the people at Chelmsford, that it was more than an houre ere I could recover my Inne gate, where I was faine to locke myselfe in my Chamber, and pacifie them with wordes out of a window insteed of deeds: to deale plainely I was so weary, that I could dance no more.

The next morning I footed it three myle of my way toward Braintree: but returned back againe to Chelmsford, where I lay that Satterday and the next Sunday. The good cheere and kinde welcome I had at Chelmsford, was much more than I was willing to entertaine: for my onely desire was to refraine drinke, and be temperate in my dyet.

At Chelmsford a Mayde not passing fourteene yeares of age, dwelling with one Sudley my kinde friend, made request to her Master and Dame, that she might daunce the Morrice with me in a great large roome. They being intreated, I was soone wonne, to fit her with bels, besides she would have the olde fashion with napking on her armes, and to our jumps we

8

---

fell. A whole houre she held out: but then being ready to lye downe I left her off: but thus much in her praise, I would have challenged the strongest man in Chelmsford, and amongst many I thinke few would have done so much.

The fourth dayes journey, beeing Munday
of the second weeke.

On Munday morning very early, I rid the 3. myles that I daunst the Satterday before: where alighting, my Taberer strucke up, and lightly tript forward, but I had the heaviest way that ever mad Morrice-dancer trod: yet

> With hey and ho, through thicke and thin
> the hobby horse quite forgotten,
> I follow'd as I did begin,
> although the way were rotten.

This foule way I could finde no ease in, thicke woods being on eyther side the lane: the lane likewise being full of deep holes, sometimes I skipt up to the waste: but it is an old Proverb. That it is a little comfort to the miserable to have companions, and amidst this miry way, I had some mirth by an unlookt for accident.

It was the custome of honest Country fellows my unknowne friends, upon hearing of my Pype (which might well be heard in a still morning or evening a myle) to get up and beare mee company a little way. In this foule waytwo pretty plaine youthes watcht me, and with their kindnes somewhat hindred me. One a fine light fellow would be still before me, the other ever at my heeles. At length comming to a broad plash of water and mud, which could not be avoyded, I fetcht a rise, yet fell in over the anckles at the further end. My youth that follow'd me, tooke his jump, and stuck fast in the midst, crying out to his companion, come George, call yee this dauncing, Ile go no further: for indeede hee could goe no further, till his

10

---

fellow was faine to wade and help him out. I could not chuse but laugh to see howe like two frogges they laboured: a hartye farwell I gave them, and they faintly bad God speed me, saying if I daunst that durtie way this seaven yeares againe, they would never daunce after me.

Well with much a doo I got unto Braintree by noone, tarried there Munday night and the next day: onely I daunst three miles on Tewsday, to ease my Wednesdaies journey.

If I should deny that I was welcome at Braintree, I should slander an honest crew of kind men, among whome I far'd well, slept well, and was every way well usde.

The fift dayes journey being Wednesday
of the second weeke.

Taking advantage of my 3. miles that I had daunst ye day before, this wednesday morning I tript it to Sudbury, whether came to see a very kinde Gentleman Master Foskew, that had before travailed a foote from London to Barwick: who giving me good counsaile to observe temperate dyet for my health, and other advise to be carefull of my company, besides his liberall entertainment, departed leaving me much indebted to his love.

In this towne of Sudbury, there came a lusty tall fellow, a butcher by his profession, that would in a Morrice keepe mee com-pany to Bury: I being glad of his friendly offer, gave him thankes, and forward we did set: but ere ever wee had measur'd halfe a mile of our way, he gave me over in the plain field protesting, that if he might get a 100. pound, he would not hold out with me; for indeed my pace in dauncing is not ordinary.

As he and I were parting, a lusty Country lasse being among the people, cal'd him faint hearted lout: saying, if I had begun to daunce, I would have held out one myle though it had cost me my life. At which words many laughed. Nay saith she, if the Dauncer will lend me a leash of his belles, Ile venter to treade one mile with him myselfe. I lookt upon her, saw mirth in her eies, heard boldnes in her words, and beheld her ready to tucke up her russet petticoate, I fitted her with bels: which he merrily taking, garnisht her thicke short legs, and with a smooth brow bad the Tabrer begin. The Drum strucke, forward marcht I with my merry Mayde-marian: who shooke her fat sides: and footed it merrily to Melfoord, being a long myle. There parting with her, I gave her (besides ker skinfull of drinke) an English crowne to buy more drinke, for good wench she was in a

---

pittious heate: my kindnes she requited with dropping some dozen of short courtsies, and bidding God blesse the Dauncer, I bad her adieu: and to give her her due, she had a good eare, daunst truely, and wee parted friendly. But ere I part with her, a good fellow my friend, having writ an odde Rime of her, I will make bold to set it downe.

> A Country Lasse browne as a berry,
> Blith of blee in heart as merry,
> Cheekes well fed and sides well larded,
> Every bone with fat flesh guarded,
> Meeting merry Kemp by chaunce,
> Was Marrian in his Morrice daunce,
> Her stump legs with bels were garnisht,
> Her browne browes with sweating varnisht:
> Her browne hips when she was lag,
> To win her ground, went swig a swag,
> Which to see all that came after,
> Were repleate with mirthfull laughter.
> Yet she thumpt it on her way,
> With a sportly hey de gay,
> At a mile her daunce she ended,
> Kindly paide and well commended.

At Melford, divers Gentlemen met mee, who brought me to one master Colts, a very kinde and worshipfull Gentleman, where I had unexpected entertainment till the Satterday. From whose house having hope somewhat to amend my way to Bury, I determined to goe by Clare, but I found it to be both farther and fouler.

The sixt dayes journey, being Satterday of the second weeke.

From Wednesday night til Satterday having bin very trouble-some, but much more welcome to master Colts: in the morning I tooke my leave, and was accompanied with many Gentlemen a myle of my way. Which myle master Colts his foole would needs daunce with me, and had his desire, where leaving me, two fooles parted faire in a foule way: I keeping on my course to Clare, where I a while rested, and then cheerfully set forward to Bury.

Passing from Clare towards Bury, I was invited to the house of a very bountifull widdow, whose husband during his life was a Yeoman of that Countrie, dying rich no doubt, as might well appeare, by the riches and plentie that abounded in every corner of the house. She is called the widdow Everet.

At her house were met above thirty Gentlemen. Such, and so plentifull variety of good fare, I have very sildome seene in any Commoners house. Her behaviour being very modest and freendly, argued her bringing up not to be rude. She was a woman of good presence: and if a foole may judge, of no smal discretion.

From this widdowes I daunst to Bury, coming in on the Sat-terday in the afternoone, at what time the right Honorable the Lord Chief Justice entred at another gate of the towne, the wondring and regardles multitude making his honor cleere way, left the streetes where he past to gape at me: the throng of them being so great, that poore Will Kemp was seaven times stayed ere hee could recover his Inne. By reason of the great snow that then fell, I stayd at Bury from Satterday in the second week of my setting foorth, til Thursday night the next weeke following.

14

The seaventh dayes journey being Friday
of the third weeke.

Upon Friday morning I set on towardes Thetford, dauncing that tenne mile in three houres: for I left Bury somewhat after seaven in the morning, and was at Thetford somewhat after ten that same forenoone. But indeed considering how I had been booted the other journeys before, and that all this way or the most of it was over a heath, it was no great wonder: for I far'd like one that had escaped the stockes and tride the use of his legs to out-run the Constable: so light was my heeles, that I counted the ten miles no better than a leape.

At my entrance into Thetford, the people came in great numbers to see mee: for there were many there, being Size time. The noble Gentleman Sir Edwin Rich, gave me entertainment in such bountifull and liberal sort, during my continuance there Satterday and Sunday, that I want fitte words to expresse the least part of his worthy usage of my unworthines: and to conclude liberally as hee had begun and continued, at my departure on Monday, his worship gave me five pound.

The eyght dayes journey being Munday
of the fourth weeke.

On Munday morning I daunst to Rockland ere I rested, and comming to my Inne, where my Hoast was a very boone companion, I desir'd to see him: but in no case he would be spoken with, till he had shifted himselfe from his working dayes sute. Being armed at all poyntes, from the cap to the codpeece, his blacke shooes shining, and made straght with copper buckles of the best, his garters in the fashion, and every garment fitting Corremsquandam (to use his own word): hee enters the Hall with his bonnet in his hand, began to crye out.

O Kemp deere Master Kemp: you are even as welcome as as as, and so stammering, he began to study for a fit comparison, and I thanke him at last he fitted me: for saith he, thou art even as welcome, as the Queenes best grey-hound. After this dogged yet well-meaning salutation, the Carrowses were called in: and my friendly Hoast of Rockland began with, All this: blessing the houre uppon his knees, that any of the Queenes Majesties well-willers or friends would vouchsafe to come within his house: as if never any such had been within his doores before.

I tooke his good meaning, and gave him great thankes for his kindnesse: and having rested mee well, began to take my course for Hingham, whether my honest Hoast of Rockland would needs be my guide: but good true fat-belly he had not followed mee two fieldes, but he lyes all along, and cryes after me to come backe and speake with him. I fulfild his request: and comming to him, dauncer quoth hee if thou daunce a Gods name God speede thee: I cannot follow thee a foote farther, but adieu good dauncer, God speed thee if thou daunce a Gods name.

16

I having haste of my way, and he being able to keep no way, there wee parted. Farewell he, he was a kinde good fellow, a true Troyan: and it ever be my lucke to meet him at more leasure, Ile make him full amendes with a Cup full of Canarie. But now I am a little better advis'd, wee must not thus let my madde hoast passe: for my friend late mentioned before, that made the odde rime on my Maide-marian, would needes remember my hoast. Such as it is Ile bluntly set downe.

> He was a man not over spare,
> In his eybals dwelt no care;
> Anon anon and welcome friend,
> Were the most words he usde to spend.
> Save sometime he would sit and tell,
> What wonders once in Bullayne fell;
> Closing each period of his tale,
> With a full cup of Nut-browne Ale.
> Turwin and Turneys siedge were hot.
> Yet all my Hoast remembers not.
> Kets field and Muscleborough fray
> Were battles fought but yesterday.
> O twas a goodly matter then
> To see your sword and buckler men;
> They would lye here and there,
> But I would meete them every where:
> And now a man is but a pricke,
> A boy armed with a poaking sticke,
> Will dare to challenge Cutting Dicke.
> O tis a world the world to see,
> But twill not mend for thee nor mee.
> By this some guest cryes ho the house,
> A fresh friend hath a fresh carouse,

Still he will drinke, and still be dry,
And quaffe with every company.
Saint Martin send him marry mates
To enter at his hostree gates:
For a blither lad than he
Cannot an Inkeeper be.

Well once againe farewell mine Hoast at Rockland: after all these farewels I am sure to Hingham I found a foule way, as before I had done from Thetford to Rockland.

Yet besides the deep way I was much hindred, by the desire people had to see me. For even as our Shop-keepers will hayle, and pull a man with Lack ye? what do you lack Gentlemen? My ware is best cryes one: mine best in England sayes an other: heere shall you have choyse saith the thirtd: so was the divers voyces of the young men and Maydens, which I should meete at everie myles ende, thronging by twentie, and sometime fortie, yea hundreths in a companie: One crying the fayrest way was thorow their Village: another, this is the nearest and fayrest way, when you have past but a myle and a halfe: an other sort crie, turne on the left hand, some on the right hand: that I was so amazed, I knewe not sometime which way I might best take: but hap hazard, the people still accompanying me, wherewith I was much comforted, though the wayes were badde: but as I said before at last I overtooke it.

The ninth dayes journey, being Wednesday
of the fourth weeke.

The next morning I left Hingham, not staying till I came to Barford-bridge, five young men running all the way with me, for otherwise my pace was not for footemen.

From Barford bridge I daunst to Norwich: but comming within sight of the Citty, perceiving so great a multitude and throng of people still crowding more and more about me, mistrusting it would be a let to my determined expedition, and pleasurable humour: which I long before conceived to delight this Citty with (so far, as my best skill, and industry of my long travelled sinewes could affoord them) I was advised, and so tooke ease by that advise, to stay my Morrice a little above Saint Giles his gate, where I tooke my gelding, and so rid into the Citty, procrastinating my merry Morrice daunce through the Citty till better opportunitie.

Being come into the Citty: Master Roger Wiler the Maior, and sundry other of his worshipfull Brethren sent for me: who perceiving how I intended not to daunce into the Citty that nyght: and being well satisfied with the reasons, they allotted me time enough not to daunce in till Satterday after: to the end that divers knights and Gentlemen, together with their wives and Children (who had beene many dayes before deceyved with expectation of my comming) might nowe have sufficient warning, accordingly by Satterday following.

In the meane space, and during my still continuaunce in the Cittye afterwardes, they not onely very courteously offered to beare mine owne charges and my followers, but very bountifully performed it at the common charges: the Mayor and many of the Aldermen often times besides invited us privately to theyr severall houses.

To make a short end of this tedious description of my entertainment: Satterday no sooner came, but I returned without the City through Saint Giles his gate: and beganne my Morrice where I left at that gate, but I entered in at Saint Stephens gate, where one Thomas Gilbert in name of all the rest of the Cittizens gave me a friendly and exceeding kind welcome: which I have no reason to omit, unlesse I would condemne my selfe of ingratitude, partlye for the private affection of the writer towardes me; as also for the generall love and favour I found in them, from the highest to the lowest, the richest as the poorest. It followes in these few lines.

Master Kemp his welcome to *Norwich*

W With hart, and hand, among the rest
E Especially you welcome are:
L Long looked for, as welcome guest,
C Come now at last you be from farre
O Of most within the Citty sure,
M Many good wishes you have had.
E Each one did pray you might indure,
W With courage good the match you made.
I Intend they did with gladsome hearts,
L Like your well willers, you to meete:
K Know you also they'l doe their parts,
E Eyther in field or house to greete
M More you then any with you came,
P Procur'd thereto with trump and fame.

Your well-willer,

T.G.

20

Passing the gate, Wifflers (such Officers as were appointed by the Mayor) to make me way through the throng of the people, which prest so mightily upon me: with great labour I got thorow that narrow preaze into the open market place. Where on the crosse, ready prepared, stood the Citty Waytes, which not a little refreshed my warines with toyling thorow so narrow a lane, as the people left me: such Waytes (under Benedicite be it spoken) fewe Citties in our Realme have the like, none better. Who besides their excellency in wind instruments, their rare cunning on the Vyoll, and Violin: theyr voices be admirable, everie one of them able to serve in any Cathedrall Church in Christendome for Quiristers.

Passing by the Market place, the presse still increasing by the number of boyes, girles, men and women, thronging more and more before me to see the end. It was the mischaunce of a homely maide, that belike, was but newly crept into the fashion of long wasted peticotes tyde with points, & had, as it seemed but one point tyed before, and comming unluckily in my way, as I was fetching a leape, it fell out that I set my foote on her skirts: the point eyther breaking or stretching, off fell her peticoate from her waste, but as chance was, thogh her smock were course, it was cleanly: yet the poore wench was so ashamed, the rather for that she could hardly recover her coate againe from unruly boies, that looking before like one that had the greene sicknesse now had she her cheekes all coloured with scarlet. I was sorry for her, but on I went towards the Maiours, and deceived the people, by leaping over the church-yard wall at S. Johns, getting so into M. Mayors gates a neerer way: but at last I found it the further way about: being forced on the Tewsday following to renew my former daunce, because George Sprat my overseer having lost me in the throng, Would not be

21

deposed that I had daunst it, since he saw me not: and I must confesse I did not wel, for the Cittizens had caused all the turn-pikes to be taken up on Satterday, that I might not be hindred. But now I returne againe to my Jump, the measure of which is to be seene in the Guild-hall at Norwich, where my buskins, that I then wore, and daunst in from London thither, stand equally devided, nailde on the wall. The plenty of good cheere at the Mayors, his bounty, and kinde usage, together with the general welcomes of his worshipful brethren, and many other knights, Ladies, Gentlemen & Gentlewomen, so much exceeded my expectation, as I adjudg'd my selfe most bound to them all. The Maior gave me five pound in Elsabeth angels: which Maior (faire Madame, to whom I too presumptuously dedicate my idle paces) as a man worthy of a singuler and impartiall admiration, if our criticke humorous mindes could as prodigally conceive as he deserves, for his chast life, liberality, & temperance in possessing worldly benefits: he lives unmarried, and childlesse, never purchased house nor land; the house he dwels in this yeere, being but hyred: he lives upon marchandies, being a Marchant venturer. If our marchants & gentlemen wold take example by this man, Gentlemen wold not sell their lands, to become banckrout Marchants, nor Marchants live in the possessions of youth-beguiled gentlemen: who cast themselves out of their parents heritages for a few outcast commodities. But wit whither wilt thou? What hath Morrice tripping Will to do with that? it keeps not time with his dance: therefore roome you morral precepts, give my legs leave to ende my Morrice, or that being ended, my hands leave to perfect this worthlesse poore tottered volume.

     Pardon me Madame, that I am thus tedious, I cannot chuse but commend sacred liberality, which makes poore

wretches partakers of all comfortable benefits, besdies the love
& favour already repeated: M. Weild the mayor gave me 40.s
yeerely during my life, making me a free man of the marchant
venturers, this is the substance of al my journey: therfore let no
man beleeve how ever before by lying ballets & rumors they
have bin abused: that either waies were laid open for me, or
that I delivered gifts to her Majesty. It is good being merry my
masters, but in a meane, & al my mirths, (meane though they
be) have bin & ever shal be imploi'd to the delight of my royal
Mistris: whose sacred ought not to be remembered among such
ribald rimes as these late thin-breecht lying Balletsingers have
proclaimed it.

It resteth now that in a word I shew, what profit I have
made by my Morrice: true it is I put out some money to have
threefold gaine at my returne, some that love me, regard my
paines, & respect their promise, have sent home the treble
worth, some other at the first sight have paide me, if I came to
seek them, others I cannot see, nor wil they willingly be found,
and these are the greater number. If they had al usd me wel, or
al ill, I would have boldly set downe the true sum of my smal
gain or losse, but I wil have patience, some few daies longer. At
the end of which time, if any be behinde, I wil draw a cattalogue
of al their names I ventur'd with: those that have shewne
themselves honest men, I wil set before them this Caracter H.
for honesty: before the other Bench-whistlers shal stand K. for
Ketlers & Keistrels, that wil drive a good companion without
need in them to contend for his owne, but I hope I shall have
no such neede. If I have, your Honorable protection shall thus
far defend your poore servant, that he may being a plain man,
call a spade a spade. Thus fearing your Ladyship is wearier with
reading this toy, then I was in all my merry travaile, I crave

pardon: and conclude this first pamphlet that ever Will Kemp offered to the Presse, being thereunto prest on the one side by the pittifull papers pasted on every poast, of that which was neither so nor so, and on the other side urg'd thereto in duety to expresse with thankefulnes the kind entertainment I found.

Your honors poore servant.

W.K.

Kemps humble request to the impudent generation of Ballad-makers and their coherents;

that it would please their rascalities to pitty his paines in the great journey he pretends, and not fill the country with lyes of his never done actes as they did in his late Morrice to Norwich.

To the tune of *Thomas Delonies* Epitaph

My notable Shakerags, the effect of my sute is discovered in the Title of my supplication. But for your better understandings: for that I know you to be a sort of witles beetle-heads, that can understand nothing, but what is knockt into your scalpes, These are by these presentes to certifie unto your block-headships, that I William Kemp, whom you had neer hand rent in sunder with your unreasonable rimes, am shortly God willing to set forward as merily as I may; whether I my selfe know not. Wherefore by the way I would wish ye, imploy not your little wits in certifying the world that I am gone to Rome, Jerusalem, Venice, or any other place at your idle appoint. I knowe the best of ye by the lyes ye writ of me, got not the price of a good hat to cover your brainles heads: If any of ye had come to me, my bounty should have exceeded the best of your good masters the Ballad-buiers, I wold have apparrelled your dry pates in party coloured bonnets, & bestowed a leash of my cast belles to have crown'd ye with cox-combs. I have made a privie search, what private Jigmonger of your jolly number, hath been the Author of these abhominable ballets written of me: I was told it was the great ballet-maker **T.D. alias Tho. Deloney,** Chronicler of the memorable lives of the 6. yeomen of the west, Jack of Newbery, the Gentle-craft, & such like honest men: omitted by Stow, Hollinshead, Grafton, Hal, froysart, & the rest of those wel deserving writers: but I was given since to understand, your late generall Tho. dyed poorely, as ye all must do, and was honestly buried: which is much to bee doubted of some of you. The

25

quest of inquiry finding him by death acquited of the Inditement, I was let to wit, that another Lord of little wit, one whose imployment for the Pageant, was utterly spent, he being knowne to be Eldertons immediate heyre, was vehemently suspected: but after due inquisition was made, he was at that time knowne to live like a man in a mist, having quite given over the mistery. Still the search continuing, I met a proper upright youth, onely for a little stooping in the shoulders: all hart to the heele, a penny Poet whose first making was the miserable stolne story of Macdoel, or Macdobeth, or Macsomewhat: for I am sure a Mac it was, though I never had the maw to see it: & hee tolde me there was a fat filthy ballet-maker, that should have once been his Journeyman to the trade: who liv'd about the towne: and ten to one, but he had thus terribly abused me & my Taberer: for that he was able to do such a thing in print.

A shrewd presumption: I found him about the bank-side, sitting at a play, I desired to speake with him, had him to a Taverne, charg'd a pipe with Tobacco, and then laid this terrible accusation to his charge. He swels presently like one of the foure windes, the violence of his breath, blew the Tobacco out of the pipe, & the heate of his wrath drunke dry two bowlefuls of Rhenish wine. At length having power to speake. Name my accuser saith he, or I defye thee Kemp at the quart staffe. I told him, & all his anger turned to laughter: swearing it did him good to have ill words of a hoddy doddy, a habber de hoy, a chicken, a squib, a squall: One that hath not wit enough to make a ballet, that by *Pol* and *Aedipol*, would Pol his father, Derick his dad: doe anie thing how ill soever, to please his apish humor. I hardly beleeved, this youth that I tooke to be gracious, had bin so graceles: but I heard afterwards his mother in law was eye and eare witnes of his fathers abuse by this blessed childe on a publique stage, in a nerry Hoast of an Innes part. Yet all this while could I not find out the true ballet-maker. Till by chaunce a friend of mine puld out of his pocket a booke in

26

Latine called *Mundus Furiosus:* printed at *Cullen,* written by one of the vildest and arrantest lying Cullians that ever writ booke, his name Jansonius, who taking upon him to write an abstract of all the turbulent actions that had beene lately attempted or performed in Christendome, like an unchristian wretch, writes onely by report, partially, and scoffingly, of such whose pages shooes hee was unworthy to wipe, for indeed he is now dead: farewell he, every dog must have a day. But see the luck on't: this beggerly lying busie-bodies name, brought out the Ballad-maker: and it was generally confirmd, it was his kinsman: he confesses himselfe guilty, let any man looke on his face: if there be not so redde a colour that all the sope in the towne will not washe white, let me be turned to a Whiting as I passe betweene Dover and Callis. Well, God forgive thee honest fellow, I see thou hast grace in thee: I prethee do so no more, leave writing these beastly ballets, make not good wenches Prophetesses, for litle or no profit, nor for a six-penny matter, revive not a poore fellowes fault thats hanged for his offence: it may be thine owne destiny one day, prethee be good to them. Call up thy olde Melpomene, whose straubery quill may write the bloody lines of the blew Lady, and the Prince of the burning crowne: a better subject I can tell ye: than your Knight of the Red Crosse. So farewel, and crosse me no more I prethee with thy rabble of bald rimes, least at my returne I set a crosse on thy forehead,

that all men may know thee
for a foole.

FINIS.

William Kemp.

27

Glossary

Bavines - bundles of brushwood used for fuel.

Bench-whistlers - those who sit idly whistling on benches.

Bowd sixpences - bent coins given as tokens of good luck.

Bullayne - Boulogne, besieged and captured by the English in 1544.

City Waits - a group of five multi-skilled musicians who played for official functions in Norwich. In addition to viols and violins, they played trumpets, sackbuts, oboes and recorders and 'an old Lyzardine'. Such was their reputation that in 1589 Sir Francis Drake had borrowed the whole band to accompany him on his voyage to Portugal. Sadly only two of the five returned.

Cullions - rascals.

Deloney - Thomas Deloney, reputedly a weaver in Norwich before he took to writing ballads and pamphlets.

Derrick - a noted Tyburn hangman at this time, whence 'to derrick' means to hang.

Dy-doppers - literally small diving birds, dabchicks. The word is here used to mean evil-doers who keep themselves out of sight and pop up when least expected.

Elderton - William Elderton, a ballad-writer and notorious tippler who died in or before 1592.

Great Spoon -the Great Spoon of Ilford was reputed to hold a quart of ale.

Hostree - hostelry.

Jades - worn-out old horses.

Ketlers & keistrels - tinkers and hoverers for prey.

Kets field - Dussindale, now thought to be in the parish of Postwick, east of Norwich, where the followers of Robert Kett were defeated by the Earl of Warwick's army in 1549.

Maw - stomach, appetite.

Melpomene - the Muse of tragedy.

Mistery - craft.

Mount Surrey -the house built from the ruins of St Leonard's Priory by the Earl of Surrey, son of the third Duke of Norfolk. It was situated on Mousehold Heath and was occupied by Kett during the rebellion of 1549. In Kemp's day it was Crown property.

Muscleborough - Musselburgh, just outside Edinburgh, where Protector Somerset defeated the Scots in 1547.

Preaze - press, confined space.

Sion - near Brentford, then in Middlesex.

Size time - the time when the Assizes were held.

Trenchmore - a boisterous country dance.

Turneys - Tournai in France, successfully besieged by the English army of Henry VIII in 1513.

Turwin - Thérouanne, an engagement of 1513 in which English troops routed the French, usually known as the 'Battle of the Spurs'.

Venter - venture.

Wifflers - whifflers, attendants employed by the Mayor of Norwich to clear the path for a procession.